REV. SR. IMMACULATA

Novena to Our lady of Fatima

A Powerful prayer that makes things happen

Copyright © 2023 by Rev. Sr. Immaculata

All rights reserved. No part of this publication may be reproduced, stored or transmitted in any form or by any means, electronic, mechanical, photocopying, recording, scanning, or otherwise without written permission from the publisher. It is illegal to copy this book, post it to a website, or distribute it by any other means without permission.

First edition

*This book was professionally typeset on Reedsy.
Find out more at reedsy.com*

*To all the faithful Catholics around the world,
It is with great honor and gratitude that I dedicate this book,
"Novena to Our Lady of Fatima," to you. Your unwavering devotion
and love for Our Lady and the Catholic faith have been a source of
inspiration and strength for me and many others.*

Contents

Chapter 1	1
Novena to Our Lady of Fatima.	1
Brief history:	1
Chapter 2	7
Devotion to Our Lady of Fatima	7
- Importance of Marian Devotion	7
- The Rosary and its Connection to Fatima	9
- Pilgrimages and Feast Days	12
Chapter 3	15
Preparing for the Novena	15
- Faith, Prayer, and Penance	15
- Benefits and Purpose of a Novena	16
- How to Pray a Novena	18
Chapter 4	22
Novena to Our Lady of Fatima - Day 1	22
Meditations for Day 1	23
Chapter 5	26
Novena to Our Lady of Fatima - Day 2	26
Meditations for Day 2	27
Chapter 6	31
Novena to Our Lady of Fatima - Day 3	31
Meditations for Day 3	32
Chapter 7	35
Novena to Our Lady of Fatima - Day 4	35

Meditations for Day 4	36
Chapter 8	40
Novena to Our Lady of Fatima - Day 5	40
Chapter 9	44
Novena to Our Lady of Fatima - Day 6	44
Meditations for Day 6	45
Chapter 10	49
Novena to Our Lady of Fatima - Day 7	49
Meditations for Day 7	50
Chapter 11	54
Novena to Our Lady of Fatima - Day 8	54
Meditations for Day 8	55
Chapter 12	58
Novena to Our Lady of Fatima - Day 9	58
Meditations for Day 9	59
Chapter 13	62
Novena to our lady of Fatima Miracles.	62
Real life stories and testimonies of our lady of Fatima novena:	63
Healing of cancer:	63
Conversion of a family member:	64
Protection from harm:	64
Financial blessing:	64
Healing of a chronic condition:	65

Chapter 1

Novena to Our Lady of Fatima.

Brief history:

The Novena to Our Lady of Fatima is a devotional prayer that has become an important part of the Catholic faith, particularly in Portugal and among Portuguese-speaking communities around the world. This novena, which is nine days of prayer in honor of the Virgin Mary, dates back to the early 20th century and is closely tied to the apparitions of Mary that took place in the Portuguese town of Fatima in 1917.

We will explore the history of the Novena to Our Lady of Fatima, from the time of the apparitions to its spread and adoption around the world.

The Apparitions at Fatima

The Novena to Our Lady of Fatima is closely linked to the apparitions of Mary that took place in the town of Fatima, Portugal, in 1917. These apparitions are among the most well-known and widely recognized Marian apparitions in the Catholic

Church.

The apparitions began on May 13, 1917, when three shepherd children – Lucia dos Santos, Francisco Marto, and Jacinta Marto – reported seeing a vision of a woman "brighter than the sun" while they were tending their sheep. The woman asked the children to return to the same spot on the 13th day of each month for the next six months, promising to reveal her identity and a message each time.

In subsequent months, the children reported seeing the same vision and hearing messages from the woman, who identified herself as the "Lady of the Rosary" and urged the children to pray for the conversion of sinners and the world peace. She also revealed a series of prophesies, including the outbreak of World War II and the rise of communism.

The final apparition took place on October 13, 1917, and was witnessed by tens of thousands of people who had gathered in Fatima in response to the children's reports. During this apparition, the Lady of the Rosary revealed her identity as "Our Lady of the Rosary" and performed what became known as the "Miracle of the Sun," in which the sun appeared to dance and change colors in the sky.

The Devotion to Our Lady of Fatima

Following the apparitions, the devotion to Our Lady of Fatima began to spread rapidly, particularly in Portugal and among Portuguese-speaking communities around the world. The message of the Lady of the Rosary was seen as a call to prayer, penance, and devotion to Mary, and many Catholics took up this call with fervor.

In the years following the apparitions, the Bishop of Leiria (the diocese that includes Fatima) launched an official inquiry into the events at Fatima, interviewing the children and many witnesses and examining physical evidence. In 1930, the Bishop declared the apparitions at Fatima to be "worthy of belief," and the devotion to Our Lady of Fatima was officially approved by the Catholic Church.

One of the central devotions associated with Our Lady of Fatima is the Rosary, a traditional Catholic prayer that involves the repetition of prayers while meditating on specific events from the life of Jesus and Mary. The Lady of the Rosary urged the children to pray the Rosary every day as a means of achieving peace and the conversion of sinners, and this call to prayer has been taken up by many Catholics around the world.

Another important aspect of the devotion to Our Lady of Fatima is the pilgrimage to the Shrine of Our Lady of Fatima in Portugal. The shrine, which includes a basilica, a chapel, and other devotional spaces, was built on the site of the apparitions and attracts millions of pilgrims each year.

The Novena to Our Lady of Fatima

The Novena to Our Lady of Fatima is a nine-day prayer that has become an important part of the devotion to Our Lady of Fatima. The novena is typically prayed in the days leading up to May 13th, the anniversary of the first apparition, or in the days leading up to October 13th, the anniversary of the final apparition and the Miracle of the Sun.

The Novena to Our Lady of Fatima typically involves reciting prayers and meditating on the messages of the Lady of the Rosary. The prayers can vary depending on the tradition and the individual, but often include the Rosary, the Hail Mary, the Our Father, and the Prayer to Our Lady of Fatima.

The Novena to Our Lady of Fatima has been embraced by Catholics around the world as a means of deepening their devotion to Mary and seeking her intercession for their prayers. Many churches and parishes offer Novena services during the days leading up to the anniversary of the apparitions, and the Novena has become an important part of many Catholic communities.

Spread of the Novena to Our Lady of Fatima

The Novena to Our Lady of Fatima has been adopted by Catholics around the world, particularly in Portugal and among Portuguese-speaking communities. However, the devotion to Our Lady of Fatima has also spread to other parts of the world, including the United States, Latin America, and Africa.

One of the key factors in the spread of the Novena to Our Lady of Fatima has been the availability of resources and materials to help Catholics pray the Novena. These resources can include prayer books, pamphlets, and online resources, which have made it easier for Catholics to learn about the devotion and incorporate it into their prayer life.

In addition, the popularity of the Novena to Our Lady of Fatima has been fueled by the continued relevance of the messages of the Lady of the Rosary. The call to prayer, penance, and devotion to Mary remains as relevant today as it was in 1917, and many Catholics have found comfort and inspiration in these messages.

CHAPTER 1

The Novena to Our Lady of Fatima has also been embraced by Catholic organizations and movements. For example, the World Apostolate of Fatima, also known as the Blue Army, was founded in 1947 with the mission of promoting the message of Our Lady of Fatima and encouraging the devotion to Mary. The Blue Army has played a key role in spreading the Novena to Our Lady of Fatima around the world and continues to be an important promoter of the devotion.

The Novena to Our Lady of Fatima is a devotional prayer that has become an important part of the Catholic faith, particularly in Portugal and among Portuguese-speaking communities around the world. The Novena is closely tied to the apparitions of Mary that took place in Fatima in 1917, and reflects the messages of the Lady of the Rosary, including the call to prayer, penance, and devotion to Mary.

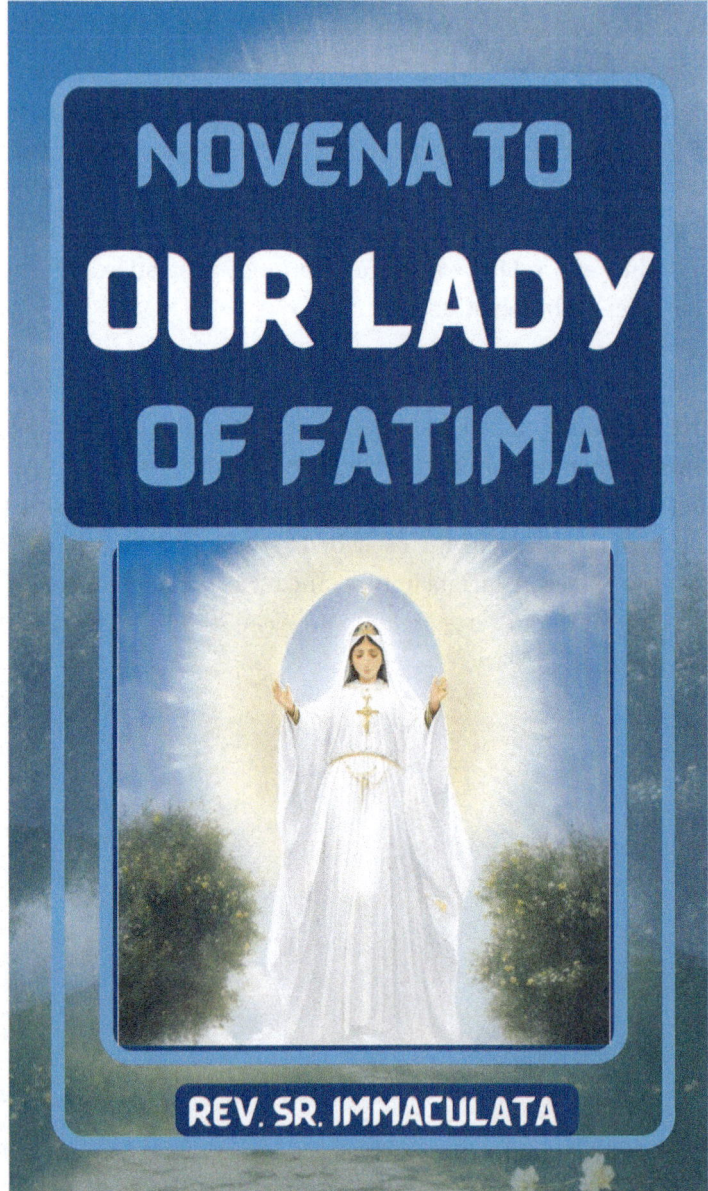

Chapter 2

Devotion to Our Lady of Fatima

- Importance of Marian Devotion

Devotion to the Blessed Virgin Mary holds a significant place within the Catholic faith, and it takes on a special meaning and relevance in the context of Our Lady of Fatima. Understanding the importance of Marian devotion allows us to appreciate the profound role Mary plays in the lives of believers and the messages she conveys through her apparitions.

1. Mary as Mother and Intercessor:

Central to Marian devotion is the recognition of Mary as the Mother of God and the Mother of the Church. Throughout history, Mary has been venerated and revered as the chosen vessel through whom God entered into human history. Her pivotal role in the incarnation of Jesus Christ makes her a beloved figure to Christians worldwide.

Moreover, devotion to Mary also stems from the belief in her powerful intercessory role. As a loving and compassionate mother, Mary cares deeply for her children and desires their spiritual well-being. Just as she interceded at the wedding at Cana, where she urged Jesus to perform his first miracle, she continues to intercede for us before her Son in heaven. This understanding of Mary's intercessory power strengthens our bond with her and encourages us to turn to her in times of need.

2. Mediation of Graces:

Marian devotion emphasizes Mary's unique role as the Mediatrix of All Graces. It is believed that she possesses a special closeness to God and acts as a channel through which divine graces flow to humanity. Through her constant intercession, Mary obtains for us the spiritual gifts and blessings we seek from God.

In the case of Our Lady of Fatima, Mary appeared to three shepherd children, delivering messages of great importance for the world. Her role as a mediator of graces was evident in her request for the devotion of the Five First Saturdays, which promised graces of repentance, conversion, and peace to those who practiced it with sincerity. This aspect of Marian devotion at Fatima underscores the belief in Mary's ability to obtain spiritual favors and lead us closer to God.

3. Immaculate Conception and Assumption:

The dogmas of the Immaculate Conception and the Assumption of Mary further emphasize the significance of Marian devotion. The Immaculate Conception affirms that Mary, from the moment of her conception, was preserved from the stain of original sin. This unique privilege bestowed upon her by God underscores her purity and holiness, making her an exemplar of faith and virtue.

Likewise, the Assumption of Mary teaches that she was taken body and soul into heaven at the end of her earthly life. This dogma acknowledges her special place in salvation history and elevates her as the Queen of Heaven. Devotion to Mary acknowledges her exalted status and inspires believers to seek her intercession with confidence.

The importance of Marian devotion, particularly in the context of Our Lady of Fatima, lies in recognizing Mary's role as a loving mother and powerful intercessor. Devotion to Mary opens avenues for spiritual growth, deepens our relationship with God, and allows us to receive abundant graces. By embracing this devotion, we honor and emulate the virtues displayed by Mary, drawing closer to her Son and embracing the transformative power of her maternal love.

- The Rosary and its Connection to Fatima

The Rosary holds a special significance in the devotion to Our Lady of Fatima, as it is intimately connected to the messages and requests Mary conveyed during her apparitions. The importance of the Rosary in the Fatima apparitions highlights its role as a powerful prayer and a means of deepening our spiritual connection with Mary and her Son, Jesus.

1. Mary's Call to Pray the Rosary:

During her appearances at Fatima, Mary consistently emphasized the importance of praying the Rosary as a means of obtaining peace and salvation for the world. She specifically requested that the children and all believers engage in the daily recitation of the Rosary.

Through this request, Mary demonstrated her confidence in the efficacy of this prayer and its ability to bring about spiritual transformation. The Rosary serves as a vehicle for contemplating the life of Jesus and Mary, fostering a deeper understanding of their divine mysteries and allowing individuals to enter into a more profound union with God.

2. Meditation on the Mysteries:

The Rosary consists of four sets of mysteries: the Joyful Mysteries, the Sorrowful Mysteries, the Glorious Mysteries, and the Luminous Mysteries. Each set of mysteries invites us to reflect on key moments in the lives of Jesus and Mary, enabling us to enter more fully into the mysteries of our faith.

In the context of Our Lady of Fatima, the Rosary serves as a pathway to meditate on the mysteries related to the lives of Jesus and Mary, including the Annunciation, the Crucifixion, the Resurrection, and the Institution of the Eucharist. Through meditative prayer, believers can immerse themselves in the events that hold profound spiritual significance and draw closer to the heart of the Gospel.

3. Spiritual Weapons and Conversion:
The Rosary is often referred to as a spiritual weapon, capable of combating evil and transforming hearts. At Fatima, Mary encouraged the faithful to employ the Rosary as a means of personal and collective conversion, offering it as a powerful tool to bring about peace in the world.

By faithfully praying the Rosary, believers engage in a spiritual battle against sin and darkness, seeking the intercession of Mary to obtain grace, mercy, and healing. The repetition of the prayers and the rhythm of the beads create an atmosphere of contemplative peace, allowing individuals to open themselves to the transformative power of God's love.

4. Association with the Fatima Apparitions:
The connection between the Rosary and the Fatima apparitions is further emphasized by the vision of the three shepherd children on October 13, 1917. During the final apparition, known as the Miracle of the Sun, the children reported seeing various religious figures, including the Blessed Virgin Mary holding a Rosary.

This manifestation not only reaffirmed the importance of the Rosary in the context of Fatima but also solidified its association with the messages and requests of Our Lady. The presence of Mary with the Rosary serves as a visible sign of her intercession and guidance, inviting believers to embrace this prayer as a pathway to spiritual renewal and conversion.

In conclusion, the Rosary is intricately connected to the devotion to Our Lady of Fatima. It serves as a powerful prayer, enabling believers to meditate on the mysteries of our faith, combat evil, and seek the intercession of Mary for peace and salvation. The Rosary holds a central place in the spiritual journey inspired by the Fatima apparitions, inviting believers to deepen their relationship with God through the loving guidance of the Blessed Virgin Mary.

- Pilgrimages and Feast Days

Pilgrimages and feast days play a significant role in the devotion to Our Lady of Fatima, offering believers the opportunity to express their faith, seek spiritual nourishment, and honor the messages and apparitions of Mary. These practices allow pilgrims and devotees to deepen their connection with Our Lady of Fatima and foster a sense of communal devotion.

1. Pilgrimages to Fatima:

Fatima, Portugal, holds immense spiritual significance as the site where the apparitions of Our Lady occurred. Pilgrims from around the world travel to Fatima to pay homage to Our Lady and seek her intercession. Pilgrimage journeys to Fatima serve as a physical and spiritual undertaking, allowing individuals to deepen their faith, seek healing, and offer prayers and penance.

Pilgrims often visit the Sanctuary of Our Lady of Fatima, which includes the Chapel of Apparitions, the Basilica, and the site of the Miracle of the Sun. They participate in religious services, processions, and devotional practices, such as the Stations of the Cross and the praying of the Rosary. The pilgrimage experience provides a unique opportunity for believers to immerse themselves in the atmosphere of devotion, unity, and reverence that Fatima inspires.

2. Feast Days of Our Lady of Fatima:

Feast days dedicated to Our Lady of Fatima are celebrated by the Catholic Church to honor the apparitions and messages of Mary. The most prominent feast day is May 13th, which commemorates the first apparition of Our Lady to the shepherd children. On this day, special Masses, processions, and devotional activities take place in Fatima and in Catholic communities worldwide.

Another significant feast day is October 13th, which marks the final apparition and the Miracle of the Sun. This date holds particular importance as it signifies the culmination of the apparitions and the confirmation of their authenticity. Devotees gather to commemorate this day with Masses, prayer vigils, and the reenactment of the apparition events.

Feast days offer believers an opportunity to reflect on the messages of Fatima, deepen their devotion to Our Lady, and recommit themselves to living out the call to prayer, penance, and conversion that Mary conveyed. These celebrations serve as moments of spiritual renewal and communal worship, uniting the faithful in their shared devotion to Our Lady of Fatima.

In conclusion, pilgrimages to Fatima and the observance of feast days associated with Our Lady of Fatima are integral components of the devotion inspired by the apparitions. They provide avenues for believers to express their faith, seek spiritual nourishment, and honor the messages of Mary. Through pilgrimages and feast day celebrations, devotees experience a sense of communal devotion and participate in the rich tradition of faith associated with Our Lady of Fatima.

Chapter 3

Preparing for the Novena

- Faith, Prayer, and Penance

In order to fully engage in the novena to Our Lady of Fatima, it is essential to prepare our hearts and minds through cultivating a strong foundation of faith, deepening our prayer life, and embracing the practice of penance. These elements are integral to the spiritual journey leading up to the novena, enabling us to enter into a more profound and transformative experience.

1. Nurturing Faith:
Faith forms the bedrock of any spiritual practice, and it is especially crucial when embarking on a novena. It involves a firm belief in the truths of the Catholic faith, including the role of Mary as the Mother of God and her intercessory power. Nurturing faith requires regular participation in the sacramental life of the Church, engaging in scripture reading, and deepening our understanding of Church teachings.

By strengthening our faith, we open ourselves to the graces and blessings that flow through the novena to Our Lady of Fatima. Faith provides the foundation for trust in Mary's intercession and the willingness to surrender ourselves to God's will, as exemplified in the messages of Fatima.

2. Deepening Prayer Life:

Prayer is the means by which we communicate with God and enter into a personal relationship with Him. Deepening our prayer life allows us to engage more intimately with Our Lady of Fatima during the novena. It involves setting aside dedicated time for prayer, embracing various forms of prayer (such as vocal, meditative, and contemplative), and seeking moments of silence and solitude to listen for God's voice.

Within the context of the novena, the recitation of the Rosary holds a special place. It provides a structured framework for meditating on the mysteries of Christ and Mary, offering an opportunity for contemplation and supplication. In addition to the Rosary, incorporating other prayers, such as litanies, novena prayers, and personal spontaneous prayers,

- Benefits and Purpose of a Novena

A novena is a prayer practice that spans nine consecutive days, often associated with a specific intention or devotion. Engaging in a novena holds profound benefits and serves a significant purpose in the spiritual journey of believers. Understanding the power and purpose of a novena allows us to fully embrace its transformative potential.

1. Fostering Perseverance and Discipline:

The duration of nine days in a novena requires commitment, discipline, and perseverance. By engaging in a novena, we cultivate qualities of dedication and steadfastness in our spiritual life. The consistency and regularity of prayer over this period help to develop a habit of seeking God and relying on His grace throughout our journey.

2. Deepening Relationship with God:

A novena provides a dedicated period of focused prayer, allowing us to deepen our relationship with God. By setting aside nine days for intentional prayer, we create space for silence, reflection, and dialogue with the Divine. This concentrated time of prayer fosters a sense of intimacy and communion with God, enabling us to draw closer to Him and grow in our understanding of His will for our lives.

3. Seeking Specific Intentions and Petitions:

Novenas are often associated with specific intentions, such as seeking healing, guidance, or spiritual growth. They serve as a means to present our heartfelt petitions and desires before God, entrusting them to His loving care. The prolonged period of prayer allows us to surrender our intentions to God repeatedly, expressing our faith and trust in His providence.

4. Cultivating Faith and Hope:

Engaging in a novena nurtures faith and hope in our hearts. As we persevere in prayer over the course of nine days, we witness the faithfulness of God in answering our prayers. This experience strengthens our belief in God's presence and His active involvement in our lives. It instills in us a hopeful expectation that God hears our prayers and responds according to His divine wisdom and timing.

5. Embracing Spiritual Transformation:

The purpose of a novena extends beyond the fulfillment of our specific intentions. It serves as a catalyst for personal and spiritual growth. Through the process of consistent and intentional prayer, we open ourselves to the transforming power of the Holy Spirit. The novena becomes an opportunity for self-reflection, repentance, and surrender to God's will. It invites us to align our hearts with God's desires, enabling us to experience inner transformation and a deepening of our faith.

In conclusion, a novena holds significant benefits and serves a profound purpose in the spiritual journey of believers. It fosters perseverance, deepens our relationship with God, allows us to present specific intentions, cultivates faith and hope, and facilitates spiritual transformation. By embracing the practice of a novena, we invite God to work in our lives, trusting in His loving guidance and responding to His invitation to draw near to Him.

- How to Pray a Novena

Praying a novena involves a structured and intentional approach to prayer over a period of nine consecutive days. While there can be variations in specific prayers and devotions depending on the intention or devotion associated with the novena, the following general steps outline how to pray a novena:

1. Set Your Intention: Determine the specific intention or purpose for which you are praying the novena. It could be seeking healing, guidance, or any other specific need or spiritual goal.

2. Choose a Novena: Select a novena that aligns with your intention or devotion. There are numerous traditional novenas available, such as the Novena to Our Lady of Fatima or the Novena to the Sacred Heart of Jesus. You can also create a personalized novena with specific prayers and readings.

3. Gather Prayers: Collect the prayers and resources needed for the novena. This may include specific prayers, readings from Scripture, or devotional materials associated with the chosen novena. You can find pre-written novena prayers in prayer books, online resources, or devotionals dedicated to specific saints or devotions.

4. Set Aside Time: Dedicate a specific time each day for the duration of the novena for focused prayer. Find a quiet and comfortable place where you can be free from distractions and create a prayerful atmosphere.

5. Open with an Invocation: Begin the novena with an invocation, expressing your desire to draw near to God and seek His guidance, mercy, or intervention according to your intention. You can use a traditional opening prayer or offer your own heartfelt words.

6. Pray the Specific Prayers: Follow the structure of the novena by reciting the specific prayers designated for each day. This may include prayers, reflections, or meditations associated with the chosen devotion or intention. The prayers may consist of vocal prayers, such as the Our Father, Hail Mary, or Glory Be, as well as other devotional prayers or novena-specific prayers.

7. Meditate and Reflect: Take time during the novena to meditate on the prayers, readings, or intentions. Reflect on their meaning and allow God to speak to your heart. Engage in contemplative prayer, seeking a deeper understanding of your intention and the presence of God in your life.

8. Conclude with a Closing Prayer: At the end of each day's prayers, conclude with a closing prayer that expresses gratitude, trust, and surrender to God's will. Offer your intentions and petitions once again, placing them in God's hands.

9. Repeat for Nine Consecutive Days:

Repeat the steps outlined above for each of the nine consecutive days of the novena. Maintain consistency and perseverance in your prayer practice, trusting in God's timing and response.

10. Express Gratitude: At the conclusion of the novena, express gratitude to God for the opportunity to seek His presence and for His faithfulness throughout the nine days of prayer. Acknowledge His sovereignty and trust in His loving care for your intentions.

Remember, the structure and specific prayers of a novena may vary depending on the chosen devotion or intention. Adapt

CHAPTER 3

the steps accordingly, while maintaining the core elements of intentionality, perseverance, and trust in God's providence throughout the nine-day period of prayer.

Chapter 4

Novena to Our Lady of Fatima - Day 1

In the name of the Father, and of the Son, and of the Holy Spirit. Amen.

O Most Holy Virgin Mary, you came to Fatima to tell three young shepherd children about the blessings that result from reciting the Holy Rosary. Give us a genuine love for this devotion so that, like the shepherd children, it is not a laborious task but a prayer that gives us life. Please help us to grow closer to your Son, Our Lord Jesus Christ, through our prayers and reflections on the mysteries of our redemption.

Like the children of Fatima, we want to bring God's word to others. Give us the strength, O Lord, to overcome our doubts so that we may be messengers of the Gospel. We know that Jesus lives in our hearts and we receive Him in the Eucharist.

Lord Jesus, the miracles, prophecies and prayers that Your Mother brought to us at Fatima amazed the whole world. We are certain of her closeness to You. We ask through the intercession of Our Lady of Fatima that you graciously hear and answer our prayers.

Especially... (Mention your intentions here...)

- Our Lady of Fatima, Pray for us!
- Our Lady of the Rosary, Pray for us!
- Immaculate Heart of Mary, Pray for us!
- "From famine and war, deliver us."
- Amen.
- In the name of the Father, and of the Son, and of the Holy Spirit. Amen.

Meditations for Day 1

1. Reflect on the Importance of Prayer: Begin your meditation by contemplating the significance of prayer in the messages of Our Lady of Fatima. Ponder how prayer can transform our hearts, bring us closer to God, and align us with His will. Consider the role of prayer in your own life and the ways in which it can deepen your relationship with God.

2. Meditate on the First Apparition: Recall the events of May 13, 1917, when Our Lady first appeared to the three shepherd children in Fatima. Visualize the scene and imagine yourself present as Mary revealed herself to Lucia, Francisco, and Jacinta. Reflect on the awe and wonder they must have experienced in the presence of the Mother of God.

3. Embrace the Call to Conversion: Contemplate the message of Our Lady of Fatima, which emphasized the importance of conversion and repentance. Examine your own life and identify areas where you can strive for greater holiness and turn away from sin. Consider the ways in which you can align your life with the teachings of Christ and the Gospel.

4. Seek Mary's Intercession: Turn to Our Lady of Fatima and entrust your intentions and needs to her intercession. Humbly ask her to intercede for you before her Son, Jesus, and to obtain for you the graces you need for your spiritual journey. Express your trust in her motherly care and her desire to help all her children.

5. Close with a Prayer: Conclude your meditation with a prayer, expressing your gratitude to Our Lady of Fatima for her presence in your life and for her intercession. Offer your intentions once again and ask for the strength to live according to God's will. End with the Hail Mary or any other prayer dedicated to Our Lady of Fatima.

Remember, these meditations are meant to guide and inspire your prayer. Feel free to adapt them according to your personal reflection and connection with Our Lady of Fatima.

CHAPTER 4

Chapter 5

Novena to Our Lady of Fatima - Day 2

✝ In the name of the Father, and of the Son, and of the Holy Spirit. Amen.

O Most Holy Virgin Mary, you came to Fatima to tell three young shepherd children about the blessings that result from reciting the Holy Rosary. Give us a genuine love for this devotion so that, like the shepherd children, it is not a laborious task but a prayer that gives us life. Please help us to grow closer to your Son, Our Lord Jesus Christ, through our prayers and reflections on the mysteries of our redemption.

Our Lady of Fatima, we pray that we may be like you and follow your example. We pray for all those who face oppression, that they will find peace. We pray and give thanks for all the blessings we enjoy.

Lord Jesus, the miracles, prophecies and prayers that Your Mother brought to us at Fatima amazed the whole world. We are certain of her closeness to You. We ask through the intercession of Our Lady of Fatima that you graciously hear and answer our prayers.

Especially... (Mention your intentions here...)

- Our Lady of Fatima, Pray for us!
- Our Lady of the Rosary, Pray for us!
- Immaculate Heart of Mary, Pray for us!
- "From nuclear war, from incalculable self-destruction, from every kind of war, deliver us."
- Amen.
- In the name of the Father, and of the Son, and of the Holy Spirit. Amen.

Meditations for Day 2

1. **Reflect on the Power of the Rosary:** Begin your meditation by contemplating the significance of the Rosary in the messages of Our Lady of Fatima. Consider the power of this prayer as a means of meditation on the life of Jesus and Mary, and as a source of strength and protection in our spiritual journey.

2. **Meditate on the Second Apparition:** Recall the second apparition of Our Lady of Fatima, which took place on June 13, 1917. Visualize the scene and imagine yourself standing alongside Lucia, Francisco, and Jacinta as they received the

loving presence of the Blessed Virgin Mary. Reflect on the message of peace and the call to pray the Rosary for peace in the world.

3. Embrace the Gift of Peace: Contemplate the urgent need for peace in our lives, families, communities, and the world. Reflect on the turmoil, conflicts, and divisions that exist and the role that prayer, especially the Rosary, can play in bringing about true and lasting peace. Consider how you can actively contribute to promoting peace in your own actions and relationships.

4. Pray the Rosary: Spend time praying the Rosary, following the joyful, sorrowful, or glorious mysteries, depending on the liturgical season. As you recite each Hail Mary, reflect on the mysteries and allow them to deepen your understanding of the life and teachings of Jesus and Mary. Offer each decade of the Rosary for specific intentions, including peace in the world.

5. Seek Mary's Intercession: Turn to Our Lady of Fatima and ask for her intercession in obtaining peace for yourself and for the world. Humbly present your prayers for peace and unity, both in your personal life and in the broader global context. Entrust your intentions to Mary's loving care, knowing that she intercedes for us before her Son.

6. Close with a Prayer: Conclude your meditation with a prayer, expressing your gratitude to Our Lady of Fatima for her guidance and intercession. Ask her to continue to lead you closer to her Son and to help you be an instrument of peace in the world. End with the Hail Mary or any other prayer dedicated to Our Lady of Fatima.

CHAPTER 5

Take time to reflect on these meditations and allow them to guide your prayer and contemplation throughout the day. Feel free to adapt them to your own personal reflection and connection with Our Lady of Fatima.

NOVENA TO OUR LADY OF FATIMA

Chapter 6

Novena to Our Lady of Fatima - Day 3

In the name of the Father, and of the Son, and of the Holy Spirit. Amen.

O Most Holy Virgin Mary, you came to Fatima to tell three young shepherd children about the blessings that result from reciting the Holy Rosary. Give us a genuine love for this devotion so that, like the shepherd children, it is not a laborious task but a prayer that gives us life. Please help us to grow closer to your Son, Our Lord Jesus Christ, through our prayers and reflections on the mysteries of our redemption.

Our Lady of Fatima, Today, we pray for an end to the suffering and injustice that plague so many parts of the world. Through the power of the Lord, you performed a miracle at Fatima and made the sun dance for thousands of people to see. Please intercede for those who are suffering.

Lord Jesus, the miracles, prophecies and prayers that Your

Mother brought to us at Fatima amazed the whole world. We are certain of her closeness to You. We ask through the intercession of Our Lady of Fatima that you graciously hear and answer our prayers.

Especially... (Mention your intentions here...)

- Our Lady of Fatima, Pray for us!
- Our Lady of the Rosary, Pray for us!
- Immaculate Heart of Mary, Pray for us!
- "From sins against the life of man from its very beginning, deliver us."
- Amen.
- In the name of the Father, and of the Son, and of the Holy Spirit. Amen.

Meditations for Day 3

1. Reflect on the Message of Repentance: Begin your meditation by contemplating the central theme of repentance in the messages of Our Lady of Fatima. Reflect on the importance of acknowledging our sins, seeking forgiveness, and embracing a life of conversion. Consider the call to repentance as a means of drawing closer to God and experiencing His mercy.

2. Meditate on the Third Apparition: Recall the third apparition of Our Lady of Fatima, which took place on July 13, 1917. Visualize the scene and imagine yourself standing with Lucia, Francisco, and Jacinta as they witnessed the powerful vision of hell. Reflect on the urgency of Our Lady's message to repent and make reparation for sin.

3. Examine Your Heart: Take time to examine your own heart and conscience. Reflect on any areas of your life where you may have strayed from God's commandments or fallen into sin. Consider the ways in which you can make amends, seek forgiveness, and strive for a more virtuous and holier life.

4. Embrace the Sacrament of Reconciliation: Contemplate the importance of the sacrament of reconciliation in the process of repentance and conversion. Consider making a sincere confession, acknowledging your sins before God, and receiving His forgiveness and healing grace. Reflect on the transformative power of this sacrament in restoring your relationship with God and others.

5. Seek Mary's Intercession: Turn to Our Lady of Fatima and ask for her intercession as you embark on the journey of repentance and conversion. Seek her guidance and assistance in recognizing your sins, seeking forgiveness, and growing in holiness. Trust in her maternal love and intercession to help you overcome obstacles and stay committed to a life of repentance.

6. Close with a Prayer: Conclude your meditation with a prayer, expressing your gratitude to Our Lady of Fatima for her role in leading you closer to her Son and helping you on the path of repentance. Ask for her continued intercession and the strength to resist temptation and embrace a life of ongoing conversion.

End with the Hail Mary or any other prayer dedicated to Our Lady of Fatima.

Take time to reflect on these meditations and allow them to guide your prayer and examination of conscience throughout the day. Embrace the call to repentance and seek God's forgiveness, trusting in His mercy and the intercession of Our Lady of Fatima.

Chapter 7

Novena to Our Lady of Fatima - Day 4

In the name of the Father, and of the Son, and of the Holy Spirit. Amen.

O Most Holy Virgin Mary, you came to Fatima to tell three young shepherd children about the blessings that result from reciting the Holy Rosary. Give us a genuine love for this devotion so that, like the shepherd children, it is not a laborious task but a prayer that gives us life. Please help us to grow closer to your Son, Our Lord Jesus Christ, through our prayers and reflections on the mysteries of our redemption.

Our Lady of Fatima, let us pray today for humility to seek forgiveness for our sins and make amends for our misdeeds.

Lord Jesus, the miracles, prophecies and prayers that Your Mother brought to us at Fatima amazed the whole world. We are certain of her closeness to You. We ask through the intercession of Our Lady of Fatima that you graciously hear and answer our prayers.

Especially... (Mention your intentions here...)

- Our Lady of Fatima, Pray for us!
- Our Lady of the Rosary, Pray for us!
- Immaculate Heart of Mary, Pray for us!
- "From hatred and from the demeaning of the dignity of the children of God, deliver us."
- Amen.
- In the name of the Father, and of the Son, and of the Holy Spirit. Amen.

Meditations for Day 4

1. Reflect on the Call to Eucharistic Adoration: Begin your meditation by contemplating the importance of Eucharistic adoration in the messages of Our Lady of Fatima. Reflect on the deep love and reverence she showed for the Eucharistic presence of Jesus and the invitation to spend time in adoration and communion with Him.

2. Meditate on the Fourth Apparition: Recall the fourth apparition of Our Lady of Fatima, which took place on August 19, 1917. Visualize the scene and imagine yourself standing with Lucia, Francisco, and Jacinta as they experienced the powerful vision of Jesus, Mary, and Joseph blessing the world. Reflect on the message of the Holy Family and their example of love and devotion.

3. Contemplate the Real Presence of Jesus: Take time to reflect on the profound mystery of the Real Presence of Jesus in the Eucharist. Ponder the gift of His body, blood, soul, and divinity that is truly present in the consecrated host. Consider the depth of love and intimacy that Jesus desires to share with us through this sacrament.

4. Embrace Eucharistic Adoration: Contemplate the invitation to spend time in Eucharistic adoration, where you can encounter Jesus in a profound and intimate way. Reflect on the peace, healing, and spiritual nourishment that can be found in His presence. Consider making regular visits to the Blessed Sacrament and opening your heart to the graces that flow from this sacred encounter.

5. Seek Mary's Intercession: Turn to Our Lady of Fatima and ask for her intercession in deepening your love and devotion to the Eucharist. Seek her guidance in approaching the Eucharist with reverence, awe, and a sincere desire for union with Jesus. Ask her to help you grow in your appreciation of this sacrament and to lead you closer to her Son through Eucharistic adoration.

6. Close with a Prayer: Conclude your meditation with a prayer, expressing your gratitude to Our Lady of Fatima for her example and intercession in nurturing your love for the Eucharist. Ask for her continued guidance and the grace to approach the Eucharist with a heart filled with love, faith, and adoration. End with the

Hail Mary or any other prayer dedicated to Our Lady of Fatima.

Take time to reflect on these meditations and allow them to guide your prayer and devotion throughout the day. Embrace the call to spend time in Eucharistic adoration and seek the intercession of Our Lady of Fatima to deepen your love for the Eucharist and your union with Jesus.

CHAPTER 7

Chapter 8

Novena to Our Lady of Fatima - Day 5

In the name of the Father, and of the Son, and of the Holy Spirit. Amen.

O Most Holy Virgin Mary, you came to Fatima to tell three young shepherd children about the blessings that result from reciting the Holy Rosary. Give us a genuine love for this devotion so that, like the shepherd children, it is not a laborious task but a prayer that gives us life. Please help us to grow closer to your Son, Our Lord Jesus Christ, through our prayers and reflections on the mysteries of our redemption.

Our Lady of Fatima, may we offer everything we do today to our Lord. As we make this offering, we think of people who are affected by our actions each day. We ask God to help us be motivated by love and compassion.

Lord Jesus, the miracles, prophecies and prayers that Your Mother brought to us at Fatima amazed the whole world. We are certain of her closeness to You. We ask through the intercession of Our Lady of Fatima that you graciously hear and answer our prayers.

Especially... (Mention your intentions here...)

- Our Lady of Fatima, Pray for us!
- Our Lady of the Rosary, Pray for us!
- Immaculate Heart of Mary, Pray for us!
- "From every kind of injustice in the life of society, both national and international, deliver us."
- Amen.
- In the name of the Father, and of the Son, and of the Holy Spirit. Amen.

Meditations for Day 5

1. **Reflect on the Virtue of Humility:** Begin your meditation by contemplating the virtue of humility as exemplified by Our Lady of Fatima. Reflect on Mary's humble acceptance of God's plan for her life and her willingness to serve Him and others with selflessness and obedience. Consider how you can cultivate greater humility in your own thoughts, words, and actions.

2. **Meditate on the Fifth Apparition:** Recall the fifth apparition of Our Lady of Fatima, which took place on September 13, 1917. Visualize the scene and imagine yourself standing with Lucia, Francisco, and Jacinta as they witnessed the miracle of the

sun. Reflect on the humility and trust with which the children approached this extraordinary event.

3. Embrace the Spirit of Humility: Contemplate the importance of humility in your spiritual journey. Reflect on any areas of pride, self-centeredness, or attachment to worldly recognition that may hinder your relationship with God and others. Consider the freedom and peace that come from embracing humility and surrendering your will to God's.

4. Practice Humility in Daily Life: Reflect on practical ways to practice humility in your daily life. Consider how you can serve others with a humble heart, listen attentively to others' needs, and seek opportunities to put others before yourself. Embrace acts of humility, such as admitting mistakes, seeking reconciliation, and accepting constructive feedback.

5. Seek Mary's Intercession: Turn to Our Lady of Fatima and ask for her intercession in cultivating the virtue of humility. Seek her guidance and assistance in imitating her humility and in overcoming pride and self-centeredness. Ask for her intercession to help you become more like her Son, who humbled Himself for the sake of humanity.

6. Close with a Prayer: Conclude your meditation with a prayer, expressing your gratitude to Our Lady of Fatima for her example of humility and for her intercession in your life. Ask for her continued guidance and the grace to embrace humility more fully. End with the Hail Mary or any other prayer dedicated to Our Lady of Fatima.

CHAPTER 8

Take time to reflect on these meditations and allow them to guide your prayer and actions throughout the day. Embrace the call to cultivate humility and seek the intercession of Our Lady of Fatima to help you grow in this virtue.

Chapter 9

Novena to Our Lady of Fatima - Day 6

In the name of the Father, and of the Son, and of the Holy Spirit. Amen.

O Most Holy Virgin Mary, you came to Fatima to tell three young shepherd children about the blessings that result from reciting the Holy Rosary. Give us a genuine love for this devotion so that, like the shepherd children, it is not a laborious task but a prayer that gives us life. Please help us to grow closer to your Son, Our Lord Jesus Christ, through our prayers and reflections on the mysteries of our redemption.

Our Lady of Fatima, sometimes we live in fear and we are too afraid to let go of our anxieties. We want to be God's instruments to achieve His will and to bring Him glory. Today we ask through your intercession, that Jesus help us to trust in Him like the children at Fatima.

Lord Jesus, the miracles, prophecies and prayers that Your

CHAPTER 9

Mother brought to us at Fatima amazed the whole world. We are certain of her closeness to You. We ask through the intercession of Our Lady of Fatima that you graciously hear and answer our prayers.

Especially... (Mention your intentions here...)

- Our Lady of Fatima, Pray for us!
- Our Lady of the Rosary, Pray for us!
- Immaculate Heart of Mary, Pray for us!
- "From readiness to trample on the commandments of God, deliver us."
- Amen.
- In the name of the Father, and of the Son, and of the Holy Spirit. Amen.

Meditations for Day 6

1. Reflect on the Virtue of Charity: Begin your meditation by contemplating the virtue of charity as demonstrated by Our Lady of Fatima. Reflect on Mary's selfless love and care for others, particularly the shepherd children to whom she appeared. Consider how you can imitate her charity by extending love and compassion to those around you.

2. Meditate on the Sixth Apparition: Recall the sixth apparition of Our Lady of Fatima, which took place on October 13, 1917.

Visualize the scene and imagine yourself standing with Lucia, Francisco, and Jacinta as they witnessed the extraordinary Miracle of the Sun. Reflect on the deep love and concern Our Lady showed for the salvation of souls.

3. Embrace a Spirit of Charity: Contemplate the importance of charity in your own life. Reflect on how you can cultivate a spirit of selflessness, kindness, and generosity towards others. Consider ways in which you can serve and support those in need, both materially and spiritually, following the example of Our Lady of Fatima.

4. Extend Love and Mercy: Reflect on the opportunities you have to extend love and mercy to others. Consider how you can show compassion, forgiveness, and understanding in your relationships and interactions. Reflect on the transformative power of love and mercy in healing wounds and fostering unity.

5. Seek Mary's Intercession: Turn to Our Lady of Fatima and ask for her intercession in developing a heart full of charity. Seek her guidance in becoming more selfless, loving, and compassionate in your thoughts, words, and actions. Ask for her intercession in extending charity to all those you encounter, especially those in most need.

6. Close with a Prayer: Conclude your meditation with a prayer, expressing your gratitude to Our Lady of Fatima for her example of charity and for her intercession in your life. Ask for her continued guidance and the grace to love others as Christ loves us. End with the Hail Mary or any other prayer dedicated to Our Lady of Fatima.

Take time to reflect on these meditations and allow them to guide your prayer and interactions throughout the day. Embrace the call to cultivate charity and seek the intercession of Our Lady of Fatima to help you grow in this virtue.

NOVENA TO OUR LADY OF FATIMA

Chapter 10

Novena to Our Lady of Fatima - Day 7

In the name of the Father, and of the Son, and of the Holy Spirit. Amen.

O Most Holy Virgin Mary, you came to Fatima to tell three young shepherd children about the blessings that result from reciting the Holy Rosary. Give us a genuine love for this devotion so that, like the shepherd children, it is not a laborious task but a prayer that gives us life. Please help us to grow closer to your Son, Our Lord Jesus Christ, through our prayers and reflections on the mysteries of our redemption.

Our Lady of Fatima, show us how to pray always. Teach us how to speak to God as a friend. Help us to make time for silence in our hectic days so that we may listen to what God has to tell us. Throughout the business of our days, help us remember God and have our hearts centered on Him.

Lord Jesus, the miracles, prophecies and prayers that Your

Mother brought to us at Fatima amazed the whole world. We are certain of her closeness to You. We ask through the intercession of Our Lady of Fatima that you graciously hear and answer our prayers.

Especially... (Mention your intentions here...)

- Our Lady of Fatima, Pray for us!
- Our Lady of the Rosary, Pray for us!
- Immaculate Heart of Mary, Pray for us!
- "From attempts to stifle in human hearts the very truth of God, deliver us."
- Amen.
- In the name of the Father, and of the Son, and of the Holy Spirit. Amen.

Meditations for Day 7

1. Reflect on the Virtue of Obedience: Begin your meditation by contemplating the virtue of obedience as exemplified by Our Lady of Fatima. Reflect on Mary's complete trust and obedience to God's will, even in the face of great challenges and uncertainties. Consider how you can cultivate a spirit of obedience in your own life.

2. Meditate on the Seventh Apparition: Recall the seventh apparition of Our Lady of Fatima, which took place on September

13, 1917. Visualize the scene and imagine yourself standing with Lucia, Francisco, and Jacinta as they witnessed the powerful message of Our Lady. Reflect on the importance of obedience in responding to God's call.

3. Surrender Your Will to God: Take time to reflect on your own willingness to surrender your will to God's. Examine areas of your life where you may struggle with obedience and submission. Consider the freedom and peace that come from trusting in God's plan and aligning your will with His.

4. Embrace God's Will: Contemplate the beauty and goodness of God's will for your life. Reflect on how you can discern and embrace His will in your daily decisions, actions, and relationships. Consider the blessings and graces that flow from aligning your life with God's perfect plan.

5. Seek Mary's Intercession: Turn to Our Lady of Fatima and ask for her intercession in fostering a spirit of obedience in your life. Seek her guidance and assistance in discerning God's will and in faithfully carrying it out. Ask for her intercession to help you surrender your will to God's with trust and humility.

6. Close with a Prayer: Conclude your meditation with a prayer, expressing your gratitude to Our Lady of Fatima for her example of obedience and for her intercession in your life. Ask for her continued guidance and the grace to align your will with God's. End with the Hail Mary or any other prayer dedicated to Our Lady of Fatima.

Take time to reflect on these meditations and allow them to

guide your prayer and actions throughout the day. Embrace the call to cultivate obedience and seek the intercession of Our Lady of Fatima to help you grow in this virtue.

CHAPTER 10

Chapter 11

Novena to Our Lady of Fatima - Day 8

In the name of the Father, and of the Son, and of the Holy Spirit. Amen.

O Most Holy Virgin Mary, you came to Fatima to tell three young shepherd children about the blessings that result from reciting the Holy Rosary. Give us a genuine love for this devotion so that, like the shepherd children, it is not a laborious task but a prayer that gives us life. Please help us to grow closer to your Son, Our Lord Jesus Christ, through our prayers and reflections on the mysteries of our redemption.

Our Lady of Fatima, today we pray for your Son to come to our aid and end the suffering and wars throughout the world. Help us to be like the children at Fatima; loving, trusting and faithful. May we pray to bring peace to our own world in our own small way by choosing to love and trust in the Lord.

Lord Jesus, the miracles, prophecies and prayers that Your Mother brought to us at Fatima amazed the whole world. We are certain of her closeness to You. We ask through the intercession of Our Lady of Fatima that you graciously hear and answer our prayers.

Especially... (Mention your intentions here...)

- Our Lady of Fatima, Pray for us!
- Our Lady of the Rosary, Pray for us!
- Immaculate Heart of Mary, Pray for us!
- "From the loss of awareness of good and evil, deliver us."
- Amen.
- In the name of the Father, and of the Son, and of the Holy Spirit. Amen.

Meditations for Day 8

1. Reflect on the Power of the Holy Spirit: Begin your meditation by contemplating the power and presence of the Holy Spirit in the messages of Our Lady of Fatima. Reflect on the role of the Holy Spirit in guiding and transforming our lives, and in empowering us to live as faithful disciples of Christ.

2. Meditate on the Eighth Apparition: Recall the eighth apparition of Our Lady of Fatima, which took place on December 10, 1925, when Our Lady appeared to Lucia in her convent. Visualize the scene and imagine yourself present as Our Lady presented the devotion of the First Saturday to Lucia and revealed the promises associated with it.

3. Open Yourself to the Holy Spirit: Reflect on the ways in which you can open your heart and life to the working of the Holy Spirit. Consider areas where you may need the Holy Spirit's guidance, strength, and wisdom. Ponder how you can cooperate with the Spirit's promptings in your daily life.

4. Embrace the Devotion of the First Saturday: Contemplate the devotion of the First Saturday, which Our Lady of Fatima asked for as a means of making reparation for the sins committed against her Immaculate Heart. Reflect on the significance of this devotion and the promises attached to it. Consider incorporating the First Saturday devotion into your spiritual life.

5. Pray for the Gifts of the Holy Spirit: Reflect on the seven gifts of the Holy Spirit: wisdom, understanding, counsel, fortitude, knowledge, piety, and fear of the Lord. Pray for an increase in these gifts in your life. Ask the Holy Spirit to strengthen you and help you live a life rooted in faith, hope, and love.

6. Seek Mary's Intercession: Turn to Our Lady of Fatima and ask for her intercession in obtaining the gifts and graces of the Holy Spirit. Ask for her guidance in growing in holiness and in becoming more open to the workings of the Holy Spirit. Trust in her motherly care and intercession as you strive to live a life filled with the Holy Spirit.

7. Close with a Prayer: Conclude your meditation with a

prayer, expressing your gratitude to Our Lady of Fatima for her intercession and for the gift of the Holy Spirit. Ask for her continued guidance and the grace to be receptive to the Holy Spirit's presence and promptings. End with the Hail Mary or any other prayer dedicated to Our Lady of Fatima.

Take time to reflect on these meditations and allow them to guide your prayer and actions throughout the day. Embrace the call to open yourself to the power of the Holy Spirit and seek the intercession of Our Lady of Fatima in obtaining the gifts and graces of the Spirit.

Chapter 12

Novena to Our Lady of Fatima - Day 9

In the name of the Father, and of the Son, and of the Holy Spirit. Amen.

O Most Holy Virgin Mary, you came to Fatima to tell three young shepherd children about the blessings that result from reciting the Holy Rosary. Give us a genuine love for this devotion so that, like the shepherd children, it is not a laborious task but a prayer that gives us life. Please help us to grow closer to your Son, Our Lord Jesus Christ, through our prayers and reflections on the mysteries of our redemption.

Our Lady of Fatima, thank you for appearing to the children at Fatima and delivering messages that are still relevant to us today. We pray again and again for peace in the world and for an end to war. May we continue to pray and sacrifice as you requested.

Lord Jesus, the miracles, prophecies and prayers that Your

Mother brought to us at Fatima amazed the whole world. We are certain of her closeness to You. We ask through the intercession of Our Lady of Fatima that you graciously hear and answer our prayers.

Especially... (Mention your intentions here...)

- Our Lady of Fatima, Pray for us!
- Our Lady of the Rosary, Pray for us!
- Immaculate Heart of Mary, Pray for us!
- "From sins against the Holy Spirit, deliver us."
- Amen.
- In the name of the Father, and of the Son, and of the Holy Spirit. Amen.

Meditations for Day 9

1. Reflect on the Triumph of the Immaculate Heart: Begin your meditation by contemplating the triumph of the Immaculate Heart of Mary, as foretold in the messages of Our Lady of Fatima. Reflect on the ultimate victory of love, goodness, and truth over sin and darkness. Consider the hope and joy that come from entrusting ourselves to the Immaculate Heart of Mary.

2. Meditate on the Ninth Apparition: Recall the ninth apparition of Our Lady of Fatima, which took place on October 13, 1917. Visualize the scene and imagine yourself standing with Lucia,

Francisco, and Jacinta as they witnessed the culmination of the Fatima messages with the Miracle of the Sun. Reflect on the profound impact this event had on the witnesses and on the world.

3. Embrace the Message of Fatima: Contemplate the messages of Our Lady of Fatima and their relevance in your life today. Reflect on the call to conversion, prayer, penance, and devotion to the Immaculate Heart of Mary. Consider how you can incorporate these messages into your daily life and strive to live them more fully.

4. Renew Your Commitment: Reflect on your own response to the messages of Fatima. Assess how well you have embraced the call to conversion, prayer, and penance. Renew your commitment to live a life of faith, hope, and love, following the example of Our Lady of Fatima.

5. Seek Mary's Intercession: Turn to Our Lady of Fatima and ask for her intercession in obtaining the graces necessary to live out the messages of Fatima. Ask for her guidance and protection in your spiritual journey. Entrust yourself and your intentions to her loving care, knowing that she desires to lead you closer to her Son.

6. Close with a Prayer: Conclude your meditation with a prayer, expressing your gratitude to Our Lady of Fatima for her intercession and for the messages she brought to the world. Ask for her continued guidance and the grace to live a life rooted in faith, hope, and love. End with the Hail Mary or any other prayer dedicated to Our Lady of Fatima.

CHAPTER 12

Take time to reflect on these meditations and allow them to guide your prayer and actions throughout the day. Embrace the call to live the messages of Fatima and seek the intercession of Our Lady of Fatima in your journey of faith and may God bless you as you follow these meditations.

Chapter 13

Novena to our lady of Fatima Miracles.

The Novena to Our Lady of Fatima is a powerful spiritual practice that has been known to bring about many miraculous outcomes for those who pray it with faith and devotion. Here are some of the miracles that have been attributed to the intercession of Our Lady of Fatima through the Novena:

Healing of physical ailments: Many people have reported being healed of physical ailments such as cancer, heart disease, and other chronic conditions after praying the Novena to Our Lady of Fatima.

1. **Conversion of sinners**: The Novena has been known to bring about the conversion of people who were previously living in sin or away from the Catholic faith. Many people have reported a deepening of their faith and a greater commitment to living a holy life after praying the Novena.
2. **Protection from harm:** People have reported being protected from harm and danger after praying the Novena

to Our Lady of Fatima. This includes protection from accidents, natural disasters, and even attacks from evil forces.
3. **Financial blessings**: Many people have reported receiving financial blessings after praying the Novena to Our Lady of Fatima. This includes unexpected windfalls, new job opportunities, and even the resolution of long-standing financial problems.
4. **Peace in families**: The Novena has been known to bring about peace and reconciliation in families that were previously torn apart by conflict and strife. Many people have reported that their relationships with family members were healed after praying the Novena.

Real life stories and testimonies of our lady of Fatima novena:

Here are some real-life stories and testimonies of the miracles attributed to the Novena to Our Lady of Fatima:

Healing of cancer:

A woman named Maria was diagnosed with stage 4 cancer and was given only a few months to live. Her family prayed the Novena to Our Lady of Fatima for her healing, and on the ninth day of the novena, Maria's cancer went into remission. She is now cancer-free and attributes her healing to the intercession of Our Lady of Fatima.

Conversion of a family member:

A man named John had a brother who had been away from the Catholic faith for many years. John prayed the Novena to Our Lady of Fatima for his brother's conversion, and on the ninth day of the novena, his brother had a profound spiritual experience that brought him back to the Catholic Church.

Protection from harm:

A family was traveling on a highway when their car suddenly started to swerve out of control. As they were about to crash, the mother shouted out to Our Lady of Fatima for help. Miraculously, their car came to a stop just inches from a concrete barrier, and the family was unharmed. They attribute their protection to the intercession of Our Lady of Fatima.

Financial blessing:

A man named Luis had been struggling financially for many years and was about to lose his home. He prayed the Novena to Our Lady of Fatima for financial assistance, and on the ninth day of the novena, he received an unexpected inheritance from a distant relative. This inheritance was enough to save his home and get him back on his feet.

CHAPTER 13

Healing of a chronic condition:

A woman named Sarah had been suffering from a chronic condition for many years and had tried everything to find relief. She prayed the Novena to Our Lady of Fatima for healing, and on the ninth day of the novena, she felt a sudden wave of warmth and peace wash over her. From that day forward, her symptoms gradually improved until she was completely healed.

These are just a few examples of the many miracles that have been attributed to the intercession of Our Lady of Fatima through the Novena. It is a powerful spiritual practice that has the potential to bring about incredible blessings and transformations in the lives of those who pray it with faith and devotion.

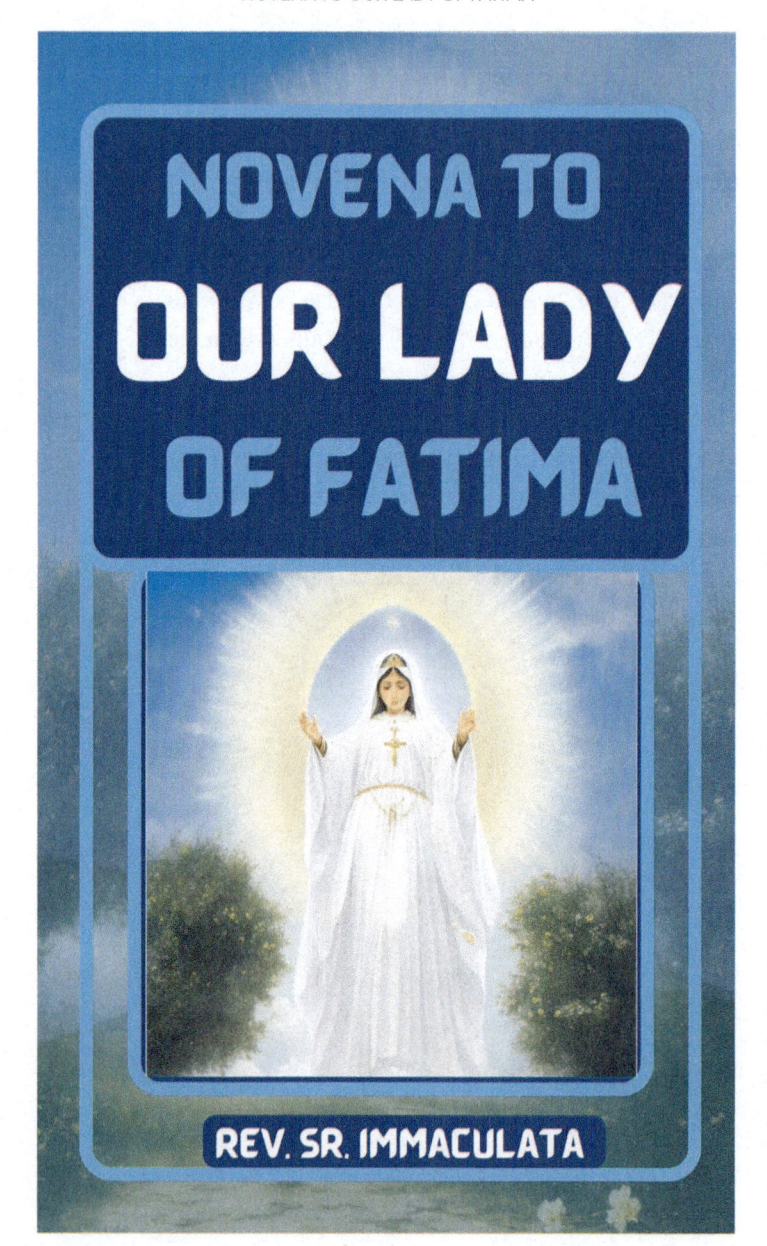

NOVENA TO OUR LADY OF FATIMA

REV. SR. IMMACULATA

Printed in Great Britain
by Amazon